SILLY JOKES & RIDDLES

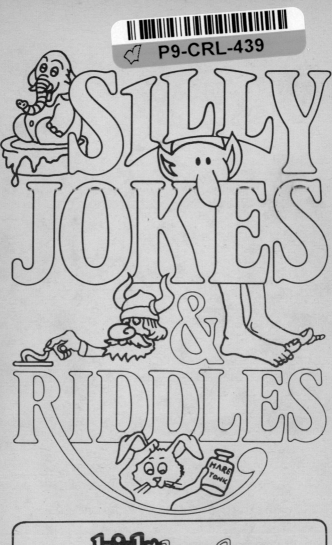

kidsbooks
Incorporated

KIDSBOOKS, INCORPORATED
7004 N. CALIFORNIA AVE.
CHICAGO, IL 60645
U.S.A.

ISBN 0-942025-32-6

MANUFACTURED IN THE UNITED STATES OF AMERICA.

What kind of music do witches play on their pianos?

Hagtime.

Why can only very small elves
live under toadstools?

Because there is not mushroom.

Which detective takes bubble baths?

Sherlock Foams.

What Indian tribe had the most lawyers?

The Sioux.

What bellows,
"Eef if of
muf?"

*A backward
giant.*

What did they call kittens in the West?

Posse cats.

What do you give bald rabbits?

Hare tonic.

**Why does a
nasty Russian
called Alf
stay indoors
when it rains?**

Because rude Alf, the Red, knows rain dear.

Why are they not growing bananas any longer?

Because they are long enough already.

Why can't you send letters to Washington any more?

Because he's dead.

What is the best way to avoid falling hair?

Jump out of the way.

Which play did Shakespeare write for baby pigs?

Hamlet.

What do sad fir trees do?

They pine a lot.

What happens when you put snakes on a car window?

You get windshield vipers.

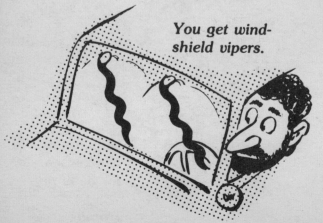

Why did the carpenter get tired of his work?

He got board.

Why did the window say, "Ouch?"

It had a pane.

13

**What did one
raisin say to
the other raisin?**

*Nothing. Raisins
can't talk.*

Who was Ivanhoe?

A Russian gardner.

What's a hindu?

It lays eggs.

What is Beethoven doing in his coffin?

He's decomposing.

What did the French pastry say to the fresh bread?

"You've got a lot of crust."

Which detective used to be an electrician?

Sherlock Ohms.

**What was the elephant
doing on the highway?**

About 2½ miles per hour.

Why can't two
elephants go
into the
swimming
pool at the
same time?

*Because they
only have one
pair of trunks.*

What is brown, hairy and coughs?

A coconut with a sore throat.

What is bright yellow and dangerous?

Shark infested custard.

What is long, orange and shoots rabbits?

A double-barreled carrot.

Where do you find baby soldiers?

In the infantry.

What do you call an Italian lost in a Scottish mist?

A Roman in the gloamin'.

Why don't elephants ride bicycles?

Because their thumbs can't work the bells.

What is round, purple, and used to rule the world?

Alexander the Grape.

What American president lived beside the sea and ate people?

Jaws Washington.

What would you call a giant legal shark?

The chief jawstice.

What do South Americans call their local mountains?

Handy Andes.

How does a fox feel after
he has eaten a duck?

Down in the mouth.

What floats, weighs
250,000 tons, and
tastes of tomato
soup?

A soupertanker.

Why does lightning shock people?

Because it doesn't know how to conduct itself.

What has pretty wings, sits on flowers, and is deadly?

A man-eating butterfly.

What leaves foot prints all over the ocean floor?

A lemon sole.

What does the Queen do when she burps?

Issues a royal pardon.

What do gorillas sing at Christmas time?

*"Jungle Bells.
Jungle Bells."*

What did one toe say to the other toe?

"Don't look now, but there are a couple of heels following us."

What is a fiord?

A Norwegeian motor car.

Why is it dangerous to play cards in the jungle?

Because of all the cheetahs.

Who is Santa Claus' wife?

Mary Christmas.

What do reindeer say before they tell a joke?

"This one will sleigh you."

What did Vikings use for secret messages?

The Norse code.

What begins with P,
ends in E, and has
a thousand letters?

Post office.

What happens
when you cross
a dog with
a giraffe?

*You get a pet
that barks at
airplanes.*

How do scientists calculate the weight of whales?

They take them to a whale weigh station.

Who was the most famous Arabian playwright?

Sheikspeare.

What is Italian, 182 feet high, and delicious?

The Leaning Tower of Pizza.

What do cats read every morning?

Mewspapers.

Who has eight guns and terrorizes the ocean?

Billy the squid.

Why do soldiers like autumn?

Because of all the leaves.

What lies at the bottom of the sea and shivers?

A nervous wreck!

How many bricks go into a house?

None. They all have to be carried.

Why do tennis players have such a good life?

They have a real racket.

What is bright yellow, weighs a ton, has four legs, and sings?

Two half-ton canaries.

What goes zzub, zzub, zzub?

A bee flying backwards.

How do you catch monkeys?

Hang from a tree and make a noise like a banana.

Why can you dive
from 300 feet
right into a
soda pop without
hurting yourself?

*Because it is
a soft drink.*

What do you call pigs who write letters?

Pen pals.

What happens when you cross an ape man with a tiger?

You get a Tarzan stripes forever.

What do you use to cut through giant waves?

A sea saw.

**What did they call the first
Scotsman?**

Mac Adam.

**What do the
animals read
in zoos?**

Gnuspapers.

**Why didn't the young moth cry,
no matter how hard he was spanked?**

*Because it is very difficult
to make a mothbawl.*

**What is a
caterpillar?**

*A worm rich
enough to buy
a fur coat.*

Where do frogs leave their hats?

In a croakroom.

What is green, curly, and plays pop music?

A transistor lettuce.

What do you get from nervous cows?

Milk shakes.

What is the most common illness among spies?

A code in the nose.

Which fish
wears spurs and
a cowboy hat?

Billy the Cod.

How would you describe a wild party at a camping site?

Intense excitement.

What happens when you cross a cement mixer with a hen?

You get a brick layer.

Why didn't the two worms go into Noah's ark in an apple?

Because everyone had to go in pairs.

Why was the sheep arrested on the highway?

It made a ewe turn.

What did the bull sing to the cow?

"When I fall in love it will be for heifer."

Heard about the exhausted kangaroo?

He was out of bounds.

Why do cows in Switzerland wear bells?

Because their horns don't work.

Who is Tibetan, hairy, and courageous?

Yak the Giant Killer.

Can an orange box?

No, but a tomato can.

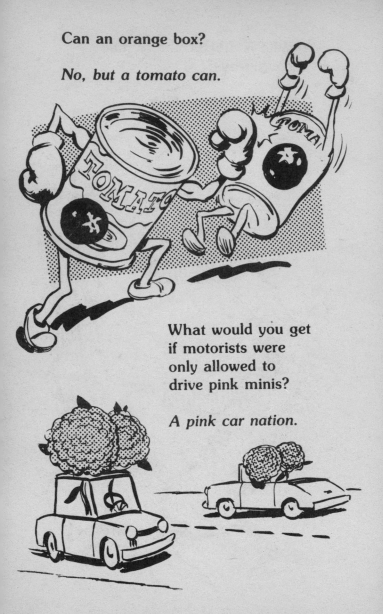

What would you get
if motorists were
only allowed to
drive pink minis?

A pink car nation.

Where do farmers leave their pigs when they come into town?

At porking meters.

53

Hear about the dancer who became a spy?

His phone was tapped.

If buttercups are yellow, what color are hiccups?

Burple.

What is gray, has four legs and a trunk?

A mouse going on a holiday.

What goes "Woof woof. Tick tick."?

A watch dog.

What do you call an elf that lives with your grannie?

An old folk's gnome

Where do astronauts leave their space ships?

At parking meteors.

What is green, curly, and religious?

Lettuce pray.

What do fish in the South Pacific sing?

"Salmon chanted evening."

What builds nests down pits?

Miner birds.

Who has huge antlers and wears white gloves?

Mickey Moose.

Why do people carry umbrellas?

Because umbrellas can't walk.

What do you get when you cross Irish midgets with ice cream cones?

Lepracones.

Why was the unemployed doctor angry?

He had no patients.

What do you get when you cross a bell with a bee?

A humdinger.

What kind of ship did Dracula captain?

A blood vessel.

What moves around a bus at 1,000 mph?

A lightning conductor.

What do policemen say to men with three heads?

"Hello. Hello. Hello."

Who wears long underwear and glitters?

Long John Silver.

What do you do with a sick wasp?

Take it to the waspital.

What do you get when you pour hot water down rabbit holes?

Hot cross bunnies.

What shows do ghosts like best at the theatre?

Phantomines.

What is brown, hairy, and limps?

A coconut with blisters.

Who was Noah's wife?

Joan of Ark.

What is brown, has 4 legs, and can see as well from either end?

A horse with its' eyes shut.

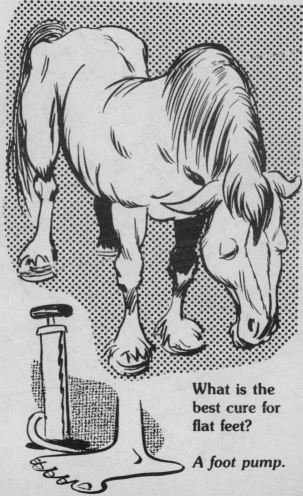

What is the best cure for flat feet?

A foot pump.

What is essential for deaf fishermen?

A herring aid.

What is a British scientist's favorite food?

Fission chips.

What do nostalgic vampires sing?

"Fangs for the memory."

What would the Swiss be without
all those mountains?

Alpless.

Hear about the
musical thief?

*He got away
with the lute.*

**How do you find out where
a flea has bitten you?**

You start from scratch.

**Who brings
Christmas presents
to police stations?**

Santa Clues.

What has six legs, is green, and deadly when it jumps at you?

An angry billiard table.

What is wild, German, and lays eggs?

Attila the Hen.

Hear about the boxing canary?

He was a featherweight champion.

How about the author who made a fortune?

He was in the write business.

Who is a vampire's favorite composer?

Bathoven.

How do you get through life with only one tooth?

You grin and bear it.

Why do devils and ghosts get along very well?

Because demons are a ghoul's best friend.

Who couldn't get their airplane to fly?

The wrong brothers.

What is big, grey, and mutters?

A mumbo jumbo.

What happens when you cross a hen with a poodle?

You get pooched eggs.

Why do vampires brush their teeth regularly?

To avoid bat breath.

Why does Dracula love to go to the races.

He loves to bat on the horses.

**What goes "Dit-dit-dot bzzz"
and then bites you?**

A morsequito.

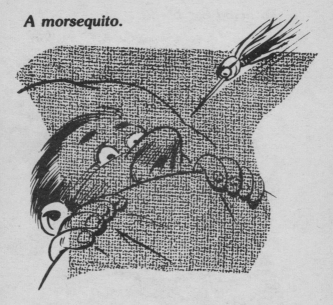

**What do you
call a pig
who tells long,
dull stories?**

*A big boar,
of course.*

Why did the Princess fall in love with the taxi?

Because it was a very handsome cab.

What did the big flower say to the little flower?

How are you, bud?

How do you get four elephants into a compact car?

Two in the front and two in the back.

How do you get four giraffes into the same compact car?

You can't until you get those elephants out!

Why do elephants paint their toenails red?

So they can hide in cherry trees.

What do vampires take for a bad cold?

Coffin drops.

What do Eskimos call big, formal dances?

Snow balls.

What do people wear to keep out the cold in China?

Ming coats.

**Why didn't the coffee cake
have many friends?**

He was crumby.

**Why was the
baker so lazy?**

*He did nothing
but loaf.*

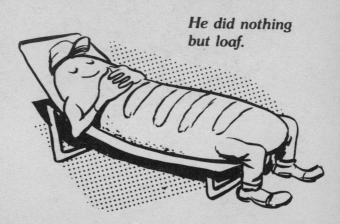

What was the baker's favorite dance?

The twist.

Why was the baker so rich?

He makes a lot of dough.

What do you call a mischievous egg?

A practical yolker.

Where do sugar fairies live?

Gnome sweet gnome.

Who is short, afraid of wolves, and uses bad language?

Little Rude Riding Hood.

**What do you call a cat
that sucks lemons?**

A sour puss.

It's sad about the human cannonball at the circus.

He got fired.

Who wrote Great Eggspectations?

Charles Chickens.

Why do bears have fur coats?

Because they would look silly in raincoats.

What do ghosts have for breakfast?

Dreaded wheat.

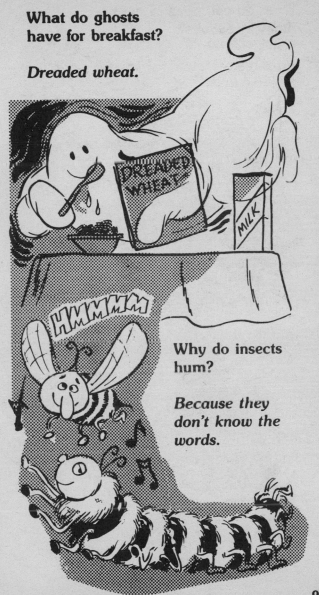

Why do insects hum?

Because they don't know the words.

What do you need to get back runaway rabbits?

Hare restorer.

What animal hibernates standing on its head?

Yoga Bear

What happens when you cross a jeep with a pet dog?

You get a land rover.

What is green, knobby, and writes essays?

A ball-point pickle.

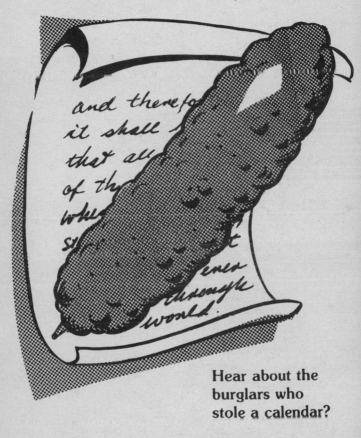

Hear about the burglars who stole a calendar?

They each got six months.